The New NASEN A–Z
of
Reading Resources

The New NASEN A–Z of Reading Resources

Suzanne Baker

David Fulton Publishers

David Fulton Publishers Ltd
The Chiswick Centre, 414 Chiswick High Road, London W4 5TF

www.fultonpublishers.co.uk
www.onestopeducation.co.uk

First published in Great Britain in 2006 by David Fulton Publishers

10 9 8 7 6 5 4 3 2 1

David Fulton Publishers is a division of Granada Learning Limited, part of ITV plc.

British Library Cataloguing in Publication Data
A catalogue record for this book is available from the British Library.

ISBN: 1 84312 441 6
EAN: 978 184312 441 2

Typeset by FiSH Books, Enfield
Printed and bound in Great Britain

Contents

Acknowledgements

The author and NASEN would like to acknowledge the role that Mike Hinson and Charles Gains played in writing and developing the original concept of the NASEN A–Z graded list of reading books.

About the Author

Suzanne Baker's lifelong interest in the acquisition of literacy arose from her classroom teaching of 5–7-year-olds, followed by extensive experience working with older children struggling to overcome their difficulties with reading and writing. A conviction that prevention was better than cure led to training as a Reading Recovery tutor. Her work with the programme for more than a decade in Dudley, Newport and Belfast resulted in her gaining a deeper understanding of the vital importance of matching the pupil to an appropriate level of text. She now carries out consultancy work for publishers and, in collaboration with Shirley Bickler she has published *Book Bands for Guided Reading: Organising Key Stage One Texts for the Literacy Hour* and *Bridging Bands for Guided Reading: Resourcing for Diversity into Key Stage 2*.

Introduction

Since the first edition of this handbook was published in 1993, the teaching of reading has continued to be a subject of constant debate, change and argument.

The introduction of the National Curriculum (NC) in 1995 clearly set out the general requirements for English at Key Stages 1–4. Within the framework it states that children should be taught to:

- read accurately, fluently and with understanding;
- understand and respond to texts they read;
- read, analyse and evaluate a wide range of texts, including literature from the English literacy heritage and from other cultures and traditions.

Since 1997 the teaching of reading has been guided by the National Literacy Strategy (NLS) and its Framework for teaching (now part of the Primary National Strategy) which sets out the teaching objectives for pupils from Reception to Year 6 to enable them to become fully literate. It emphasises that in order to become successful readers pupils need to use a range of strategies to be able to access the meaning of a text. The NLS saw the range of strategies as being like searchlights, each shedding light on to a text. Pupils need to have access to all the strategies so they can search out their own way through what they are reading.

The NLS suggests a number of strategies, including:

- Phonic (sound and spelling)
- Knowledge of content
- Grammatical knowledge
- Word recognition and graphic knowledge

The NLS places a great deal of emphasis on the teaching of phonics and the decoding of words through the pupils' knowledge of sounds and spellings. It is a concern that without this attention to how words sound and are spelt, there can be an overreliance on familiar and predictable texts and this can cause problems when attempting to decode more complex, less familiar texts.

However, the NLS in its Introduction, states:

> In the early stages, pupils should have a carefully balanced programme of guided reading from books of graded difficulty, matched to their independent reading levels. These

guided reading books should have cumulative vocabulary, sensible grammatical structure and lively and interesting content.

In April 2005, the House of Commons Education and Skills Select Committee published their report *Teaching Children to Read*. The report drew together the findings of the Committee's inquiry, which focused on the methods used in schools to teach children to read. This report called for a review of the National Literacy Strategy to determine whether its current prescriptions and recommendations are the best available methodology for the teaching of reading in primary schools.

Following this report, the Government commissioned an independent review of the teaching of reading, the interim report of which was published in December 2005: *The Rose Report – Independent Review of The Teaching of Early Reading.*

Reading Resources

While the debate continues, the need for high-quality reading resources at all levels of reading ability is the key issue for most schools. Without high quality, stimulating reading material to support the strategies that teachers are using in their classrooms, pupils will not develop their reading skills.

Clearly this guidance has implications for schools' reading resources. There is probably the best range of reading resources ever, available from a large number of highly respected and highly regarded publishing houses, many with years of experience in the 'reading book' market. Schemes published in line with the National Curriculum in the mid-1990s have since been revised and updated to meet the objectives of The National Literacy Strategy. Additional resources added (Big Books, games, CD-ROMs, pupil support materials, teaching notes) have developed to provide an inclusive package to ensure all pupils have access to as wide a range of resources to support the reading process as possible.

The cost of these resources is significant and schools, using additional funding to support the introduction of the NLS, were able to update and purchase new materials to support their teaching.

Choosing reading resources

In order that schools make the most effective use of the financial resources available, it is advisable for them to develop an annual audit process, reviewing the current reading resources and updating and renewing where necessary.

When considering new reading resources, it is preferable to examine the potential purchases either through publishers visiting the school, teachers visiting exhibitions or through the purchase of inspection/evaluation packs.

When selecting reading resources it is important to assess not only the strengths and weaknesses of a particular title or series but also to be aware of that resource's value in relation to the whole school stock. In order to reflect a balance, teachers should ask themselves if the school's reading resources include:

- An adequate range with regard to pupil reading level and pupil interest level
- A wide variety appropriate to children's different ages, abilities and reading attainments
- Books which are accessible to all pupils within the school
- Books that reflect equal opportunities and a multi-racial society

Reading resources are no longer just reading books for the pupils to use. Many of the publishing houses now provide Big Books for class activity and pupil support materials including copy-masters and games. Many resources are also supported by CD–ROMs and/or a dedicated website, and all come with extensive teacher notes.

Criteria for choosing reading resources

With the advancement in technology, children's access to learning materials has become highly sophisticated. The rapid increase in instant visual technology (television, DVD, cinema, computer games, the Internet) means that schools have to be even more aware of what reading materials are available and what criteria should be used to choose them. It is very easy for children and young people to be 'switched off' from reading at a very young age because the material they are given is dated, uninspiring and difficult to access.

The following guidance may be useful when selecting reading resources for schools:

- Will the cover design and outward appearance of the book motivate the reader to open its pages?
- Does the style and type of print, and the space between words and lines, enable the book to be easily read?
- Are the illustrations of good quality? Will they help the reader understand the text? Are they appropriate for the age of the reader?
- Is there an appropriate balance of text in relation to the illustrations?
- Is the book written in a clear style of language?
  - Does it follow a pattern of common words or does it contain many new and unfamiliar words?
  - Are there many long sentences?
  - How complex is the grammar?
  - Are the ideas clearly organised?
- If it is a fiction book:
  - Does it have a good story that will capture the reader's attention?
  - Are the characters believable?
  - Are all the characters portrayed in a sensitive way?
  - Will readers be able to identify with the story?
- If it is a non-fiction book:
  - Is the information up to date?
  - Is the subject matter sufficiently simplified without being patronising?
  - Are technical terms clearly explained?
  - Is the information easily accessible (clear contents page, index, etc.)?
- Do the pupil resource materials that accompany the books support the child's learning?
- Do the reading books and supplementary materials support the National Curriculum and the Primary and Secondary National Strategies?
- Can the resources be used by pupils working independently?

- Are the ICT resources compatible with the school's IT systems? Do they need adult supervision or can the pupils access them themselves?
- Is there guidance for parents on how the reading resources might be used at home?
- Are the resources durable and able to withstand the wear and tear of a classroom?

The NASEN A–Z List

Back in 1993, the main purpose of the *A–Z Handbook of Reading Schemes* was to facilitate choice, encourage prudent purchasing and to help the organisation of reading materials to ensure that they were effectively matched to the individual needs of young readers.

Through the National Literacy Strategy (now the Primary National Strategy and Secondary National Strategy), schools have developed effective processes to improve learning and teaching in all aspects of literacy, including reading. It has become more and more evident that as well as high-quality teaching there also needs to be an adequate and varied selection of attractive, stimulating and interesting reading materials for all levels of reading ability to ensure that effective and developmental learning takes place.

The guidance and frameworks for the teaching of reading may have developed and changed but the rationale behind this book has not. The requests by teachers for a revision of this text during the last two years has identified that there is still a need for a supportive framework for the purchase and organisation of reading books and related resources in schools.

As schools become more accountable and need to demonstrate effective best value in their purchasing strategies, it is hoped that this handbook will aid that process. This handbook should be seen as an essential tool in the appraisal of existing stock, for the purchasing of new stock and as an enabling tool to ensure that old and new stock are integrated to provide the school with a comprehensive reading library that meets the needs of all pupils.

Lorraine Peterson
Chief Executive Officer of NASEN
May 2006

Explanatory Notes

This book is intended as a resource for all teachers in primary schools, and in the special needs departments of secondary schools.

Key

T = Teacher guide available
S = Support materials available including copy-masters, etc.
BB = Big Books available
IT = supported by CD-ROM and/or dedicated website

Titles in Italics

Titles in *italics* indicate recently out-of-print series. As well as being shown in italics 'out of print' appears in the comment column. A few series are currently being phased out. These are marked as out of print and to be discontinued when stocks are exhausted. Not all titles within the series may be available.

Other Things to Note

Most of the more recent series, especially at Key Stage 2, are either linked to the National Curriculum or to the National Literacy Framework and are intended for use with specific year groups.

The *main list* is arranged by year group. The *supplementary list* is arranged in bands of interest age as given by publishers.

Publishers' estimates of *Reading Ages* (RA) or *NC levels* are given wherever available. It has not been possible to independently verify the reading age of every title. Publishers themselves rarely indicate how these have been arrived at. All reading ages should be regarded as an approximate guide only.

The notes in the comments column are for guidance or explanation and are mostly taken from publishers' own promotional materials.

Notes on the Supplementary List

Only series designated by publishers as intended for reluctant, struggling readers or older developing readers are included. Some series are stand-alone; others are linked to general series by simplified *Access* versions of the same text or differentiated text within the same book.

The A–Z of
Reading Resources

Series Title and Publisher	Features	YR/P1	Y1/P2	Y2/P3
4U2Read.OK Barrington Stoke	Fiction			
All Aboard Ginn	T, S, BB, IT Fiction	**Easy Start** 16 titles **Stage 1 Introductory** 12 titles **Stage 1** 12 titles **Stage 2** 20 titles	**Stage 3** 20 titles **Stage 4** 16 titles **Stage 5** 18 titles	**Stage 6** 8 titles **Stage 7** 8 titles **Stage 8** 8 titles
All Aboard Non-fiction Ginn	T, S, BB, IT Non-fiction strand of All Aboard	**Stage 1 Introductory** 6 titles **Stage 1** 6 titles **Stage 2** 6 titles	**Stage 3** 6 titles **Stage 4** 6 titles **Stage 5** 6 titles	**Stage 6** 6 titles **Stage 7** 6 titles **Stage 8** 6 titles
Alpha to Omega Heinemann	T, S			
Alphakids Horwitz Gardner	T Each set contains a range of fiction and non-fiction 6 titles per set	**Level 1–8** (Emergent–Early)	**Level 6–16** (Early–Transitional)	**Level 15–23** (Transitional–Extending)
Alphakids Plus Horwitz Gardner	T, S Each set contains a range of fiction and non-fiction 6 titles per set	**Level 1–8** (Emergent–Early)	**Level 6–16** (Early–Transitional)	**Level 15–23** (Transitional–Extending)

a

Y3/P4	Y4/P5	Y5/P6	Y6/P7	KS3 Older Developing Readers	Comment
← 9 titles → RA below 8		← 17 titles → RA below 8			Simplified versions of Barrington Stoke novels for reluctant readers by significant authors
Stage 9 6 titles **Stage 10** 6 titles	**Stage 10** 6 titles **Stage 11** 6 titles	**Stage 12** 6 titles **Stage 13** 6 titles	**Stage 13** 6 titles **Stage 14** 6 titles		**Out of print**
Stage 9 2 titles **Stage 10** 2 titles	**Stage 10** 2 titles **Stage 11** 2 titles	**Stage 12** 2 titles **Stage 13** 2 titles	**Stage 13** 2 titles **Stage 14** 2 titles		**Out of print**
←		Back-up readers 12 titles		→	Highly structured programme for use from KS2 to adult. Back-up Readers consolidate programme stages
Level 20–23 (Extending)					Non-fiction also useful for older developing readers
Level 20–24 (Extending)					Non-fiction also useful for older developing readers

Series Title and Publisher	Features	YR/P1	Y1/P2	Y2/P3
Alphaworld Horwitz Gardner	T, S, BB Non-fiction series 4–6 titles per pack, 94 titles	**Band 1A** Pink **Band 1B** Pink **Band 2** Red **Band 3** Yellow	**Band 3** Yellow **Band 4** Blue **Band 5** Green **Band 6** Orange **Level 12–14** Green **Level 15–16** Orange	**Band 6** Orange **Band 7** Turquoise **Band 8** Purple **Level 15–16** Orange **Level 17–18** Turquoise **Level 19–20** Purple **Level 21–22** Gold
Badger KS2 Guided Reading Badger Publishing	T, S, IT Fiction			
Badger Secondary Reading Boxes Badger Publishing	Fiction and non-fiction sets			
Bananas Egmont Books	Fiction	←——— **Green Bananas** ———→	←——— **Blue Bananas** ———→	←——— **Red**

Y3/P4	Y4/P5	Y5/P6	Y6/P7	KS3 Older Developing Readers	Comment
Level 21–22 Gold **Level 23–24** White					Also useful for older developing readers at KS2
6 titles	6 titles	6 titles	6 titles		Guided Reading support on a range of popular titles and classics
				Breakaway Fiction for Weaker Readers **Surefire Winners Novels A** **Surefire Winners Novels B** **Fantasy and Sci-fi Group Readers** **Mysteries Group Readers** RA 8–10	For weaker readers Approx 32 books per set
Bananas ⟶ ⟵———**Yellow Bananas**———⟶					A wide range of titles for independent readers

Series Title and Publisher	Features	YR/P1	Y1/P2	Y2/P3
Bangers and Mash (O/P) Longman	T, S Fiction	**Set 1–6** 6 titles ← **Set 1A–6A** 6 titles →	**Set 7–12** 6 titles **Supplementary Books** 8 titles	**Set 13–18** 6 titles
Big Cat Collins	T, S, BB, IT A range of fiction and non-fiction in each set	**Lilac** 10 titles **Pink A** 10 titles **Pink B** 10 titles **Red A** 10 titles **Red B** 10 titles **Yellow** 11 titles	**Yellow** 11 titles **Blue** 13 titles **Green** 10 titles **Orange** 10 titles	**Turquoise** 10 titles **Purple** 10 titles **Gold** 10 titles
Black Cats A&C Black	Fiction for independent readers			
Blitzit Nelson Thornes	T Fiction			
Blue Bananas Egmont Books see **Bananas**				
Book Project Longman see **Longman Book Project**				
Bookwise Nelson Thornes	T, S Fiction and non-fiction sets			

Y3/P4	Y4/P5	Y5/P6	Y6/P7	KS3 Older Developing Readers	Comment
					Phonic series **Out of print**
White 10 titles **Lime** 10 titles					Published 2005
← 34 titles →					Short chapter books for confident readers
		←	**Set A** 6 titles **Set B** 6 titles RA 8+	→	For reluctant readers
Bookwise 3 fiction pack 15 titles non-fiction pack 10 titles	**Bookwise 4** fiction pack 15 titles non-fiction pack 10 titles	**Bookwise 5** fiction pack 15 titles non-fiction pack 10 titles	**Bookwise 6** fiction pack 15 titles non-fiction pack 10 titles		**Out of print** To be discontinued when stocks are exhausted

Series Title and Publisher	Features	YR/P1	Y1/P2	Y2/P3
Brainwaves Badger Publishing				
Buzzwords Nelson Thornes	Non-fiction			
Cambridge Reading CUP	T, S, BB, IT Fiction and non-fiction sets	**Foundation Stage Phonics** 12 titles **Patterned and natural language** 18 titles **Pattern and rhyme** 18 titles **Nursery Rhymes** 6 titles	**Age 5–6 Phonics** 9 titles **Familiar Settings** 9 titles **Fantasy Worlds** 9 titles **Range of Cultures** 9 titles **Narrative Recounts** 9 titles **Poetry** 9 titles **Non-fiction** 9 titles	**Age 6–7 Phonics** 9 titles **Familiar Settings** 9 titles **Fantasy Worlds** 9 titles **Range of Cultures** 9 titles **Narrative Recounts** 9 titles **Poetry** 9 titles **Non-fiction** 9 titles
Chill Outs Horwitz Gardner	Fiction			
Chillers A&C Black	Fiction			
Colour Crackers Orchard Books	Fiction			←
Colour Jets A&C Black	Fiction			←

Y3/P4	Y4/P5	Y5/P6	Y6/P7	KS3 Older Developing Readers	Comment
				Set 1 Green 18 titles **Set 2 Orange** 18 titles **Set 3 Purple** 18 titles RA 8+ **Blue Set** 6 titles RA 6+	High interest easy-to-read non-fiction
		← **Pack A** 8 titles **Pack B** 8 titles **Pack C** 8 titles RA 8+ →			For reluctant readers
Year 3 Reading Books 12 titles	**Year 4 Reading Books** 12 titles	**Year 5 Reading Books** 12 titles	**Year 6 Reading Books** 12 titles		Revised edition
		←	15 titles RA 6.5–8.5 →		For turned-off readers
←	5 titles		→		
16 titles RA 7 →					Humorous stories Some tapes available
15 titles RA 6+ →					Suitable for reluctant readers

Series Title and Publisher	Features	YR/P1	Y1/P2	Y2/P3
Comix A&C Black	S Fiction			
Crunchies Orchard Books	Fiction			←
Crunchies – Colour Crunchies Orchard Books	Fiction			←
Crunchies – Super Crunchies Orchard Books	Fiction			
Dark Flight Badger Publishing	T, S			
Digitexts Longman	T, IT Fiction and non-fiction CDs			

Y3/P4	Y4/P5	Y5/P6	Y6/P7	KS3 Older Developing Readers	Comment
20 titles RA 7+ ←——————→					Graphic fiction boy-friendly
Crazy Camelot 8 titles **Little Horrors** 8 titles **Raps** 6 titles ———————→ **Scaredy Cats** 8 titles RA 7+					Suitable for beginner readers and older reluctant readers
Colour Crackers 16 titles **First Fairy Tales** 8 titles **Scout and Ace** ———————→ 4 titles **Titchy Witch** 8 titles RA 7+					Suitable for beginner readers and older reluctant readers
←—— **Seriously Silly Stories** ——→ 12 titles RA 7+					Suitable for newly independent readers and older reluctant readers
				10 titles RA 6.6–7	Boy-friendly
Feargal Fly Shared fiction **Extreme Weather** Shared non-fiction **Danger, Monsters, Aliens!** Guided fiction **Treasure and Treachery** Guided non-fiction	**Digimouse** Shared fiction **Extreme Habitats** Shared non-fiction **The Black Knight** Guided fiction **Ice Bricks And Straw Roofs** Guided non-fiction	**Drag n'Drop** Shared fiction **One Great Day** Shared non-fiction **Lost Boy** Guided fiction **Earth, Sun and Moon** Guided non-fiction	**The Last Mission** Shared fiction **Peak Adventures** Shared non-fiction **Skulldiggery** Guided fiction **Fields of Glory** Guided non-fiction		Interactive CDs: 2 shared texts and 2 guided texts per year containing differentiated text with Access versions

Series Title and Publisher	Features	YR/P1	Y1/P2	Y2/P3
Discovery World Heinemann	T, S, BB, IT Non-fiction		**Stage C** Core Books 4 titles Links 5 titles **Stage D** Core Books 3 titles Links 5 titles	**Stage E** Core Books 4 titles Links 5 titles **Stage F** Core Books 2 title Links 5 titles
Essentials Horwitz Gardner	T, S A range of fiction and non-fiction in each set	**Set A** High Frequency Words 30 titles	**Set B** Initial Consonant Clusters 30 titles **Set C** Final Consonant Clusters 30 titles	
Explorers Kingscourt/McGraw-Hill	T, S, IT Non-fiction			
Fact Finders OUP see **Oxford Reading Tree Non-fiction**				
Falconwood Series AMS Educational see **Turnaround**				
Fireflies OUP see **Oxford Reading Tree – 'Fireflies'**				
First Explorers Kingscourt/McGraw-Hill	T, S Non-fiction			**Set 1** ← 12 titles — RA 7–8
First Stories Horwitz Gardner	T, S A range of fiction and non-fiction in each set	**Set A–F** 10 titles per set		

Y3/P4	Y4/P5	Y5/P6	Y6/P7	KS3 Older Developing Readers	Comment
					Includes Big Books for teaching non-fiction writing
	Set 1 12 titles RA 8–9.6	Set 2 12 titles RA 9.6–10.6	Set 3 ← 12 titles → RA 10.5–12		Also suitable for older developing readers
→ Set 2 ← 12 titles → RA 7.6–8.6					Precedes Explorer's series from same Publisher
					High frequency word practice

f

Series Title and Publisher	Features	YR/P1	Y1/P2	Y2/P3
Five Minute Thrillers Hi-Lo Books LDA	T Fiction			
Four Corners Longman	T, S, IT Non-fiction	**Star Stage R** 20 titles	**Star Stage 1** 20 titles	**Star Stage 2** 20 titles
Freestyle Express Raintree	Non-fiction			
Full Flight Badger Publishing	T, S Varied genres			

Y3/P4	Y4/P5	Y5/P6	Y6/P7	KS3 Older Developing Readers	Comment
				Set 1 8 titles **Set 2** 8 titles RA 9	Tapes available for many titles
Star Stage 3 20 titles	Star Stage 4 20 titles	Star Stage 5 20 titles	Star Stage 6 20 titles		Cross-curricular non-fiction
				Material Matters 6 titles Turbulent Planet 4 titles **Energy Essentials** 4 titles **Incredible Creatures** 8 titles **Mean Machines** 4 titles **Body Talk** 6 titles **On the Front Line** 6 titles **A Painful History of Medicine** 4 titles **Destination Detectives** 6 titles RA 8	Non-fiction for reluctant readers Parallel differentiated versions of mainstream Freestyle series
		←	**Full Flight 1** 10 titles **Full Flight 2** 10 Titles **Full Flight 3** 10 Titles RA 7.5–8	→	Particularly boy-friendly

Series Title and Publisher	Features	YR/P1	Y1/P2	Y2/P3
Fuzzbuzz OUP	T, S, IT Fiction, includes a non-fiction strand			
Genre Range Longman see **Literacy Lan**d				
Gigglers Nelson Thornes	T, S, IT Fiction			←
Glow-worms OUP see **Oxford Reading Tree**				
Go Facts A&C Black	T, S Non-fiction		←——— Transport ——→	Y1–2 Packs Seasons 4 titles Transport 4 titles Food 4 titles ←
gr8reads Barrington Stoke	Fiction			
Graffix A&C Black	Fiction			

Graffix

Y3/P4	Y4/P5	Y5/P6	Y6/P7	KS3 Older Developing Readers	Comment
		Level 1, 1A, 1B 18 titles RA 5–6.6 **Level 2, 2A, 2B** 18 titles ←————— **Level 2** ————→ **fuzzbuzz facts** 6 titles RA 6–7.11 **Level 3, 3A** RA 8–9.6			A highly structured special needs scheme
Level 1 8 titles **Level 2** ←— 8 titles —→ **Level 3** 8 titles RA 6–7.6					Humorous fiction for reluctant readers
Y2–3 Pack ←— Animals —→ 4 titles **Y3–4 Pack** ←—— Plants ——→ 4 titles **Y4–5 Pack** ←—— Oceans ——→ 4 titles					Boy-friendly
				8 titles RA below 8	Tapes also available
		←———— 28 titles ————→ RA 9			Graphic novels for reluctant readers, boy-friendly

23

Series Title and Publisher	Features	YR/P1	Y1/P2	Y2/P3
Green Bananas Egmont Books see **Bananas**				
Happy Families Puffin	Fiction			← 20 titles —
High Impact Heinemann	T Separate packs of fiction, non-fiction and drama at each level			
Hi-Lo Books LDA see **Five Minute Thrillers** and **Ten Minute Thrillers**				
Hodder Reading Project Hodder Murray	T, S A range of fiction non-fiction and plays in each set			
Hotlinks Kingscourt/McGraw-Hill	T, S, IT Anthologies		←	20 titles RA 5–6.6

Y3/P4	Y4/P5	Y5/P6	Y6/P7	KS3 Older Developing Readers	Comment
→					
				Set A fiction non-fiction plays RA 6–7 **Set B** fiction non-fiction plays RA 7-8 **Set C** fiction non-fiction plays RA 8–9 **Set D** fiction non-fiction plays RA 9–10	For reluctant readers, wide range of titles and genres **Out of print** To be discontinued when current stocks are exhausted
		←	**Level 2** 6 titles NC level 2 **Level 3** 6 titles NC level 3 → **Level 4** 6 titles NC level 4 **Level 5** 6 titles NC level 5		An intensive catch-up programme
→					Brief anthologies of fiction and non-fiction

Series Title and Publisher	Features	YR/P1	Y1/P2	Y2/P3
I Can Read HarperCollins www.Icanread.com	Contains many titles currently in print		Stage 2 ← → Stage 3	
Impact Heinemann	T Separate packs of fiction, non-fiction and drama at each level			
Inclusive Readers David Fulton	T, S, BB Fiction, non-fiction and poetry titles			
Info Trail Longman see **Literacy Land**				

Y3/P4	Y4/P5	Y5/P6	Y6/P7	KS3 Older Developing Readers	Comment
Stage 4 **Stage 5**					Many titles e.g. Frog and Toad, some tapes also available
				Set A fiction non-fiction plays RA 6–7 **Set B** fiction non-fiction plays RA 7–8 **Set C** fiction non-fiction plays RA 8–9 **Set D** fiction non-fiction plays RA 9–10	For reluctant readers, wide range of titles and genres **Out of print**
3 titles	3 titles	3 titles	3 titles		Intended for pupils with moderate to severe learning difficulties; 4 levels of photocopiable text, from p scales to NC level 1, accompany each Big Book. Many aspects of disability represented

Series Title and Publisher	Features	YR/P1	Y1/P2	Y2/P3
Infosteps Kingscourt/McGraw-Hill	S, IT Non-fiction			
Interactive Literacy Ginn	T, IT	R CD	**Y1 CD Multimedia Reading CD** Level 1 3 texts	**Y2 CD Multimedia Reading CD** Level 2 3 texts
Jelly and Bean Jelly and Bean	Fiction	**Reception Series** 22 titles **The 'b' Series** 10 titles **The Pig Family Series** 10 titles	**Red C-V-C Series** 10 titles **Pig Family Blends** 6 titles **Consonants- Blends-Clusters** 14 titles ←——— **Long Vowel** ———→ **Series** 16 titles **More Vowel Series** 16 titles **Gold Series** 4 titles	
Jets Collins	Fiction			

j

Y3/P4	Y4/P5	Y5/P6	Y6/P7	KS3 Older Developing Readers	Comment
Set 1 20 titles RA 7–8	**Set 2** 20 titles RA 8–9	**Set 3** 20 titles RA 9–10	**Set 4** 20 titles RA 10–11		A website divided into 4 levels of reading difficulty to match accompanying sets of books. Also useful at KS3
Y3 CD	Y4 CD	Y5 CD	Y6 CD		Multimedia texts for whole class teaching; 1 reading CD per NC level
Multimedia ←——Reading CD——→ Level 3 3 texts		Multimedia ←——Reading CD——→ Level 4 3 texts		Multimedia Reading CD Level 5 3 texts	
					Synthetic Phonic programme
←—————— 53 titles in print RA 7+ ——————→					Independent readers

Series Title and Publisher	Features	YR/P1	Y1/P2	Y2/P3
Jolly Readers Jolly Learning	T, S Separate fiction and non-fiction sets	**Level 1 Red** Inky Mouse and Friends 6 titles General fiction 6 titles Non-fiction 6 titles **Level 2 Yellow** Inky Mouse and Friends 6 titles General Fiction 6 titles Non-fiction 6 titles	**Level 2 Yellow** Inky Mouse and Friends 6 titles General fiction 6 titles Non-fiction 6 titles **Level 3 Green** Inky Mouse and Friends 6 titles General fiction 6 titles Non-fiction 6 titles	
Jumbo Jets Collins	Fiction			← 8 titles ← RA 7+
Jumpstart Collins	T, S A range of fiction, non-fiction and poetry in each set		**Stage 1** ← Set A, B, C ——————→ 18 titles RA 5–6	**Stage 2** ← Set A, B, C 18 titles RA 6–7
Jumpstart Extra Collins	T, S Non-fiction		**Stage 1** Set A, B, C ← 10 titles ——————→ RA 5–6	**Stage 2** ← Set A, B, C 10 titles RA 6–7
Key Words with Ladybird Ladybird	S Fiction	1A, B, C 2A, B, C	3A, B, C 4A, B, C 5A, B, C	6A, B, C 7A, B, C 8A, B, C

Y3/P4	Y4/P5	Y5/P6	Y6/P7	KS3 Older Developing Readers	Comment
					Independent readers to accompany Jolly Phonics Programme
→					Independent readers
					Early intervention scheme for less confident readers
Stage 3 ← Set A, B, C 18 titles RA 7–8 →					
					Vocabulary and themes linked to Jumpstart
Stage 3 ← Set A, B, C 10 titles RA 7–8 →					
9A, B, C **10A, B, C**	**11A, B, C** **12A, B, C**			A 'look and say' series	

Series Title and Publisher	Features	YR/P1	Y1/P2	Y2/P3
Letterland Letterland International	T, S, BB, IT Tapes Fiction	**Early Readers Set 1a** 6 titles **Set 1b** 6 titles	**Early Readers Set 2a** 6 titles **Set 2b** 6 titles **Set 2c** 6 titles Letterland ← Story Books → 20 titles	
Lighthouse Ginn	T, IT A range of fiction and non-fiction in each set	**Pink A** 8 titles **Pink B** 8 titles **Red** 10 titles **Yellow** 10 titles	**Yellow** 8 titles **Blue** 8 titles **Green** 8 titles **Orange** 8 titles	**Turquoise** 8 titles **Purple** 8 titles **Gold** 8 titles **White** 8 titles
Lightning Ginn	T, S, IT A range of fiction, non-fiction, poetry and plays			
Link-up Collins	S Fiction	**Starter Books** 12 titles **Main Reader 1 Build-up Books** Sa, Sb ,Sc 1a, 1b, 1c	**Main Readers** 2, 3, 4, 5 **Build-up Books** 2a, 2b, 2c 3a, 3b, 3c 4a, 4b, 4c 5a, 5b, 5c	**Main Readers** 6, 7, 8 **Build-up Books** 6a, 6b, 6c 7a, 7b, 7c 8a, 8b, 8c
Literacy and Science Reading Packs Neate Publishing	T Non-fiction			**Animal Sets** **Body Parts** **Colours Around Us**

Y3/P4	Y4/P5	Y5/P6	Y6/P7	KS3 Older Developing Readers	Comment
					Phonic series
White 8 titles **Lime** 8 titles					Provides opportunities to develop the full range of reading strategies
8 titles	8 titles	8 titles	8 titles		Every title contains 3 texts at different reading levels
Main Readers 8, 9, 10 **Build-up Books** 8a, 8b, 8c 9a, 9b, 9c 10a, 10b, 10c					**Out of print** to be discontinued when current stocks are exhausted
Comparing Giraffes and Polar Bears ←——— A Basic Encyclopaedia ———→ of Food A Basic Dictionary of Plants and Gardening		Teeth ←——— Food Chains ———→ Digestion: What Is It?			9 titles

Series Title and Publisher	Features	YR/P1	Y1/P2	Y2/P3
Literacy Land – Genre Range Longman	T, S, BB, IT Fiction		**Beginner Readers** 15 titles	**Emergent Readers** 15 titles
Literacy Land – Info Trail Longman	T, IT Non-fiction		**Beginner Readers** 8 titles per theme	**Emergent Readers** 8 titles per theme
Literacy Land – Story Street Longman	T, S, BB, IT Fiction	**Foundation Step** 6 wordless titles **Step 1** 18 titles	**Step 2** 18 titles **Step 3** 18 titles	**Step 4** 9 titles **Step 5** 9 titles **Step 6** 9 titles
Literacy Land – Streetwise Longman	T, IT Fiction			
Literacy Links Plus Kingscourt/McGraw-Hill	T, S, IT A range of fiction and non-fiction in each set	**Level 1** (Emergent A) 24 titles **Level 2** (Emergent B) 24 titles **Level 3** (Emergent C) 24 titles	**Level 2** (Emergent B) 24 titles **Level 3** (Emergent C) 24 titles **Level 4** (Emergent D) 24 titles **Level 5** (Early A) 24 titles **Level 6** (Early B) 24 titles **Level 7** (Early C) 24 titles	**Level 6** (Early B) 24 titles **Level 7** (Early C) 24 titles **Level 8** (Early D) 24 titles **Level 9** (Fluent A) 24 titles **Level 10** (Fluent B) 24 titles

Y3/P4	Y4/P5	Y5/P6	Y6/P7	KS3 Older Developing Readers	Comment
Competent Readers 15 titles	Fluent Readers 15 titles	**Independent Readers** 6 titles 6 Access versions	**Independent Plus Readers** 6 titles 6 Access versions		Poetry, plays, letters and diaries, comics, traditional tales
Competent Readers 5 titles per theme	Fluent Readers 5 titles per theme	**Independent Readers** 2 titles per theme + Access versions	**Independent Plus Readers** 2 titles per theme + Access versions		History, geography, science themes
Step 7 6 titles **Step 8** 6 titles **Step 9** 6 titles	**Step 10** 6 titles **Step 11** 6 titles **Step 12** 6 titles				
		Short Story Collections + Access versions 3 titles **Novels** 2 titles **Access Novel** 1 title	**Short Story Collections** + Access versions 3 titles **Novels** 2 titles **Access Novel** 1 title		
Level 11 (Fluent C) 24 titles **Level 12** (Fluent D) 24 titles **Level 13** (Stage 7) Core Readers 24 titles **Level 13** Chapter Books 12 titles	Level 14 (Stage 8) Core Readers 24 titles **Level 14** Chapter Books 6 titles **Level 14** Independent Readers 6 titles	Level 15 (Stage 9) Core Readers 24 titles **Level 15** Chapter Books 18 titles **Level 15** Independent Readers 6 titles	Level 16 (Stage 10) Core Readers 24 titles **Level 16** Chapter Books 12 titles **Level 16** Independent Readers 12 titles		Each set contains texts at a range of reading levels

Series Title and Publisher	Features	YR/P1	Y1/P2	Y2/P3
Literacy World Heinemann	T, S, IT Fiction and non-fiction titles			
Literacy World Comets Heinemann	T, S Fiction			
Literacy World Satellites Heinemann	T, S Fiction and non-fiction titles			
Livewire Chillers Hodder Murray	Fiction			
Livewire Fiction Hodder Murray	Fiction			
Livewire Graphics Hodder Murray	T Fiction			
Livewire Non-Fiction Hodder Murray	Non-fiction			

Y3/P4	Y4/P5	Y5/P6	Y6/P7	KS3 Older Developing Readers	Comment
Stage 1 Fiction 5 titles Non-fiction 4 titles	**Stage 2** Fiction 5 titles Non-fiction 4 titles	**Stage 3** Fiction 5 titles Non-fiction 4 titles	**Stage 4** Fiction 5 titles Non-fiction 4 titles		
Stage 1 Fiction 4 titles	**Stage 2** Fiction 4 titles	**Stage 3** Fiction 4 titles	**Stage 4** Fiction 4 titles		Literacy World strand for more able readers.
Stage 1 Fiction 5 titles Non-fiction 4 titles	**Stage 2** Fiction 5 titles Non-fiction 4 titles	**Stage 3** Fiction 5 titles Non-fiction 4 titles	**Stage 4** Fiction 5 titles Non-fiction 4 titles		Literacy World strand for weaker readers. Non-fiction titles are simplified versions of core texts
				4 titles RA 6–7 16 titles RA 7–8 9 titles RA 8–9 3 titles RA 9–10	
				6 titles RA 6–7 6 titles RA 7–8 8 titles RA 8–9 5 titles RA 9–10	
				8 titles	Highly visual introductions to pre-20th-century literature
				2 titles RA 6–7 20 titles RA 7–8 11 titles RA 8–9 6 titles RA 9–10	

Series Title and Publisher	Features	YR/P1	Y1/P2	Y2/P3
Livewire Plays Hodder Murray	Plays			
Livewire Real Lives Hodder Murray	Biography			
Livewire Shakespeare Graphics Hodder Murray	T			
LM Chapter Books Horwitz Gardner	Fiction			**Set 1** 24 titles ← **Set 2** ── 24 titles RA 7–8.5
Longdale Park (Pathways to Literacy) Collins	T Fiction			
Longman Book Project Longman	T, S, BB Fiction, including poetry and plays	**Beginner Levels 1–3** 15 books per set	**Longman Band 1** 6 clusters 6 books per cluster **Longman Band 2** 6 clusters 6 books per cluster	**Longman Band 3** 6 clusters 6 books per cluster **Longman Band 4** 6 clusters 6 books per cluster

Y3/P4	Y4/P5	Y5/P6	Y6/P7	KS3 Older Developing Readers	Comment
Fiction Silver Level 20 titles **Non-fiction Silver Level** 6 titles					Assessment materials available
Silver Level 6 titles					Each title contains 2 versions of the same tale, 1 story and 1 playscript
Y3 Pocket Tales 9 titles **Pocket Chillers** 3 titles **Pocket Facts** 6 titles **Pocket Sci-Fi** 3 titles	**Y4 Pocket Tales** 9 titles **Pocket Chillers** 3 titles **Pocket Facts** 6 titles **Pocket Sci-Fi** 3 titles	**Y5 Pocket Tales** 9 titles **Pocket Chillers** 3 titles **Pocket Facts** 6 titles **Pocket Sci-Fi** 3 titles	**Y6 Pocket Tales** 9 titles **Pocket Chillers** 3 titles **Pocket Facts** 6 titles **Pocket Sci-Fi** 3 titles		Independent reads

P

Series Title and Publisher	Features	YR/P1	Y1/P2	Y2/P3
Rainbow Readers Ransom	T, S, IT Fiction	← 26 readers →		
Rainbow Reading Kingscourt/McGraw-Hill	T, S Fiction with tapes			←
Rapid Heinemann				
Read it Yourself Ladybird	Fiction	**Level 1** 6 titles	**Level 2** 6 titles **Level 3** 6 titles	**Level 3** 6 titles **Level 4** 6 titles
Read it Yourself Non-fiction Ladybird	Non-fiction	**Level 1** 7 titles	**Level 1** 7 titles **Level 2** 7 Titles	**Level 2** 7 titles
Read with Ladybird Ladybird	Fiction	**Books 1–6**	**Books 6–12**	**Books 12–16**
Read with Me Ladybird	S	**Starter Reader** Books 1–4	**Developing Reader** Books 5–8	**Improver Reader** Books 9–12

r

Y3/P4	Y4/P5	Y5/P6	Y6/P7	KS3 Older Developing Readers	Comment
					Each title covers one letter of the alphabet. Also suitable for developing readers throughout KS1
	White Series 20 books and tapes RA 5–6 **Red Series** 20 books and tapes RA 6–7 **Orange Series** 20 books and tapes RA 7–8 **Yellow Series** 20 books and tapes RA 8–9 **Green Series** 20 books and tapes RA 9–10 **Blue Series** 20 books and tapes RA 10–11 **Violet Series** 20 book and tapes RA 11–12				Audio-assisted learning
	6 stages for struggling readers at KS2. NC 1c–3c				To be published summer 2006
Level 4 6 titles					Tapes available
Books 16–20					
Confident Reader Books 13–16					

Series Title and Publisher	Features	YR/P1	Y1/P2	Y2/P3
Read Write Inc OUP see www.ruthmiskin.literacy.com	T, S Fiction	←	**Set 1 Green** 10 titles **Set 2 Purple** 10 titles **Set 3 Pink** 10 titles **Set 4 Orange** 12 titles **Set 5 Yellow** 10 titles **Set 6 Blue** 10 titles **Set 7 Grey** 13 titles	
Reading Packs Neate Publishing See **Literacy and Science Reading Packs**				
Reading World Longman	T Fiction	**Level 1**	**Level 2**	**Level 3**
Red Bananas Egmont Books see **Bananas**				
Rigby Navigator Rigby	T, S, IT A mixture of fiction and non-fiction			
Rigby Navigator Dimensions Rigby	T, S, IT Anthologies containing fiction and non-fiction			
Rigby Navigator Max Rigby	T, S, IT Fiction			

Y3/P4	Y4/P5	Y5/P6	Y6/P7	KS3 Older Developing Readers	Comment
					An inclusive literacy training programme for Foundation to Year 4 and pupils working below NC level 2b. Read Write Inc 2 programme now available for Y5–8.
					Out of print
Brown Band 3 fiction titles 3 non-fiction titles	**Grey Band** 3 fiction titles 3 non-fiction titles	**Blue Band** 3 fiction titles 3 non-fiction titles	**Red Band** 3 fiction titles 3 non-fiction titles		Fiction, 3 stories per title
Year 3 Teaching CD 3 anthologies	**Year 4** Teaching CD 3 anthologies	**Year 5** Teaching CD 3 anthologies	**Year 6** Teaching CD 3 anthologies		
Brown Band 3 titles	**Grey Band** 3 titles	**Blue Band** 3 titles	**Red Band** 3 titles		Lower ability guided reading catch-up programme NC level 2c–4

Series Title and Publisher	Features	YR/P1	Y1/P2	Y2/P3
Rigby Rocket Rigby	T, IT Fiction with a few non-fiction titles in each pack	**Pink** 18 titles **Red** 18 titles	**Yellow** 18 titles **Blue** 14 titles **Green** 14 titles	**Orange** 8 titles **Turquoise** 8 titles **Purple** 8 titles **Gold** 8 titles **White** 8 titles
Rigby Star Rigby	T, S, IT Fiction	**Lilac** 8 titles **Pink** 22 titles **Red** 22 titles	**Yellow** 20 titles **Blue** 14 titles **Green** 12 titles	**Orange** 6 titles **Turquoise** 6 titles **Purple** 6 titles **Gold** 6 titles **White** 6 titles
Rigby Star Quest Rigby	T, S, IT Non-fiction	**Pink** 14 titles **Red** 4 titles	**Yellow** 4 titles **Blue** 4 titles **Green** 4 titles	**Orange** 4 titles **Turquoise** 4 titles **Purple** 4 titles **Gold** 4 titles **White** 4 titles
Sails Heinemann	T Fiction	**Pink Band** **Set A** 32 titles **Set B** 32 titles **Set C** 32 titles		
Sam's Football Stories Brilliant Publications	Fiction			

S

Y3/P4	Y4/P5	Y5/P6	Y6/P7	KS3 Older Developing Readers	Comment
White 8 titles **Lime** 8 titles					Independent readers; website for parents
White 6 titles **Star Plus** 10 titles					
White 4 titles **Star Plus** 4 titles					
					24 4-book packs, each pack focusing on one high frequency word; teaching notes within each text
←————————		**Set 1** 6 titles RA 6–7 **Set 2** 6 titles RA 7–8	————————→		Boy-friendly

S

Series Title and Publisher	Features	YR/P1	Y1/P2	Y2/P3
Skyracer Collins	A range of fiction and non-fiction within each set			
Skyways Collins	T, S Fiction			
Snapdragons OUP see **Oxford Reading Tree**				

S

Y3/P4	Y4/P5	Y5/P6	Y6/P7	KS3 Older Developing Readers	Comment
Yellow 12 fiction titles 12 non-fiction titles	**Blue** 12 fiction titles 12 non-fiction titles	**Purple** 12 fiction titles 12 non-fiction titles	**Green** 12 fiction titles 12 non-fiction titles		
	Level 1 8 titles RA 6 approx **Level 2** 8 titles RA 6.6 **Level 3** 16 titles RA 7 **Level 4** 16 titles RA 7.6	**Level 5** 8 titles RA 8 **Level 6** 8 titles RA 8.6 **Level 7** 8 titles RA 9			For less able readers. New edition 1998

←————————————→ (Level 2 RA 6.6)

←————————————→ (Level 6 RA 8.6)

Series Title and Publisher	Features	YR/P1	Y1/P2	Y2/P3
Soundstart Nelson Thornes	T, S, BB, IT Mainly fiction	**Red** **Core Readers** 6 titles **Booster Readers** 6 titles **Non-fiction** 6 titles **Orange** **1 Core Reader** **Booster Readers** 6 titles **Non-fiction** 3 titles	**Yellow** **1 Core Reader** **Booster Readers** 6 titles **Non-fiction** 3 titles **Green** **1 Core Reader** **Booster Readers** 6 titles **Non-fiction** 6 titles **Blue** **1 Core Reader** **Booster Readers** 6 titles **Non-fiction** 6 titles	**Blue** **1 Core Reader** **Booster Readers** 6 titles **Non-fiction** 6 titles **Indigo** **1 Core Reader** **Booster Readers** 6 titles **Non-fiction** 6 titles **Violet** **1 Core Reader** **Booster Readers** 6 titles **Non-fiction** 6 titles
Sparklers Nelson Thornes	T, S Fiction			**Level 1** 8 titles – RA 6 approx **Level 2** 8 titles – RA 6.6 **Level 3** 8 titles – RA 7 **Level 4** 8 Titles – RA 7.6
Sports Zone Nelson Thornes	Fiction			
Spotlight on Fact Collins	T, S, BB, IT Non-fiction		**Toys and Games** 8 titles	**The Seaside** 8 titles
Spotlight on Plays Collins	T, S			3 titles

S

Y3/P4	Y4/P5	Y5/P6	Y6/P7	KS3 Older Developing Readers	Comment
					Phonic structure Plays and poetry titles also available for Blue, Indigo and Violet sets
					For reluctant readers; each level includes 1 assessment book
		←———	**Level 1** 6 titles **Level 2** 6 titles **Level 3** 6 titles RA 8+	———→	For reluctant readers
Active Earth 8 titles	**Living Together** 8 titles	**Our Environment** 8 titles	**Making a Difference** 8 titles		Focus on reading into writing; 1 CD per year
3 titles	3 titles				

S

Series Title and Publisher	Features	YR/P1	Y1/P2	Y2/P3
Spotty Zebra Nelson Thornes	T Paired fiction and non-fiction titles	**Pink A** 20 titles **Pink B** 20 titles **Red** 20 titles **Community Books** 10 titles **Artefacts** 10 titles		
Star Rigby see **Rigby Star**				
Star Quest Rigby see **Rigby Star Quest**				
Story Chest Kingscourt/McGraw-Hill	BB Fiction	**Stage 1** **Get Ready** **Sets A–C** 24 titles **Get Ready** **Sets AA–DD** 32 titles **Ready-set-go** **Sets A–D** 32 titles **Ready-set-go** **Sets AA–DD** 32 titles	**Stage 2** **Main Readers** 2 titles **Supplementary** **Readers** 4 titles **Stage 3** **Main Readers** 2 titles **Supplementary** **Readers** 4 titles	**Stage 4** **Main Readers** 2 titles **Supplementary** **Readers** 4 titles **Stage 5** **Main Readers** 2 titles **Supplementary** **Readers** 4 titles **Stage 6** **Main Readers** 2 titles **Supplementary** **Readers** 4 titles **Stage 7** **Main Readers** 2 titles **Supplementary** **Readers** 4 titles

S

Y3/P4	Y4/P5	Y5/P6	Y6/P7	KS3 Older Developing Readers	Comment
					A Foundation Stage cross-curricular programme

S

Series Title and Publisher	Features	YR/P1	Y1/P2	Y2/P3
Story Steps Kingscourt/McGraw-Hill	T, S Mostly fiction, 1 fact title in each set	**Step 1** 5 titles **Step 2** 5 titles **Step 3** 5 titles **Step 4** 5 titles **Step 5** 5 titles	**Step 6** 5 titles **Step 7** 5 titles **Step 8** 5 titles **Step 9** 5 titles **Step 10** 5 titles **Step 11** 5 titles **Step 12** 5 titles **Step 13** 5 titles **Step 14** 5 titles	**Step 15** 5 titles **Step 16** 5 titles **Step 17** 5 titles **Step 18** 5 titles **Step 19** 5 titles **Step 20** 5 titles
Story Street Longman see **Literacy Land**				
Storyteller Kingscourt/McGraw-Hill	T, S, IT A range of fiction and non-fiction in each set	**Storyteller 1** 13 titles **Storyteller 2** 26 titles **Storyteller 3** 15 titles	**Storyteller 3** 15 titles **Storyteller 4** 17 titles **Storyteller 5** 13 titles **Storyteller 6** 16 titles	**Storyteller 6** 16 titles **Storyteller 7** 14 titles **Storyteller 8** 16 titles **Storyteller 9** 18 titles **Storyteller 10** 8 titles
Storyworlds Heinemann	T, S, BB, IT Fiction	**Stage 1** 24 titles **Stage 2** 24 titles **Stage 3** 24 titles	**Stage 4** 16 titles **Stage 5** 16 titles **Stage 6** 16 titles	**Stage 7** 16 titles **Stage 8** 16 titles **Stage 9** 16 titles

S

Y3/P4	Y4/P5	Y5/P6	Y6/P7	KS3 Older Developing Readers	Comment
					Each step consists of 1 anthology and 3 little books and benchmark assessment text
Storyteller 10 8 titles **Storyteller 11** 8 titles	**Storyteller 12** 8 titles	**Storyteller 13** 8 titles	**Storyteller 14** 8 titles		
Storyworlds Bridges Stage 10 4 titles → **Stage 11** 4 titles **Stage 12** 4 titles					4 strands of stories at each stage

S

Series Title and Publisher	Features	YR/P1	Y1/P2	Y2/P3
Streetwise Longman see **Literacy Land**				
Sunshine Galaxy Paperbacks Horwitz Gardner	T, S, IT Fiction			
Sunshine Nature Books Horwitz Gardner	T, S, BB, IT Non-fiction			←
Sunshine Readers Horwitz Gardner	T, S, IT Fiction			**Orange Level** 16 titles **Light Blue Level** 16 titles **Purple Level** 16 titles
Ten Minute Thrillers LDA	T Fiction			
The News Horwitz Gardner	T, S Non-fiction			
Tommy Handsome Prints	Fiction		**Swapping Tommy**	

t

Y3/P4	Y4/P5	Y5/P6	Y6/P7	KS3 Older Developing Readers	Comment
Stage 1 16 titles	**Stage 2** 16 titles	**Stage 3** 16 titles			Also useful for older reluctant readers
Series 1 12 titles **Series 2** 13 titles **Series 3** 12 titles					
				10 titles RA 8	For struggling and reluctant readers. Some tapes also available
The News IA 10 titles **The News IB** 10 titles **The News II** 10 titles		**News Extra** 10 titles			Magazine-style format, also useful for older developing readers
					To promote inclusion for Traveller children. Series under development; for other titles especially for Travellers see www.standards. dfes.gov.uk/ ethnic minorities

Series Title and Publisher	Features	YR/P1	Y1/P2	Y2/P3
Trackers OUP	T, S, IT Fiction and non-fiction sets at each level			←
Treetops, TreeTops Non-fiction OUP see **Oxford Reading Tree**				
Tristars Horwitz Gardner	T, S Each set contains linked fiction and non-fiction titles			←
True Stories OUP see **TreeTops Non-fiction**				
Turnaround AMS Educational	S Fiction			

Y3/P4	Y4/P5	Y5/P6	Y6/P7	KS3 Older Developing Readers	Comment
	Bear Tracks 10 titles RA 5.6 approx **Elephant Tracks** 10 titles RA 5.9 **Frog Tracks** 10 titles RA 6 **Giraffe Tracks** 10 titles RA 6.3 **Parrot Tracks** 10 titles RA 6.6 **Tiger Tracks** 10 titles RA 6.9 **Zebra Tracks** 10 titles RA 7				For struggling readers working within NC level 1–2.
Tristars Stage A 15 titles **Tristars Stage B** 15 titles **Tristars Stage C** 15 titles					5 sets at each stage, each set has 1 non-fiction text, closely linked with 1 related fiction stories
				Turnaround 1 12 titles **Turnaround 2** 12 titles **Turnaround Plays Pack 1** 4 titles **Turnaround Plays Pack 2** 4 titles RA 7–9	For reluctant readers; well-known authors

Series Title and Publisher	Features	YR/P1	Y1/P2	Y2/P3
Voyage (Oxford English Voyage) OUP	T Fiction			
Wellington Square Nelson Thornes	T, S, IT Fiction and non-fiction			

W

Y3/P4	Y4/P5	Y5/P6	Y6/P7	KS3 Older Developing Readers	Comment
Voyage Y3 collection	Voyage Y4 collection	Voyage Y5 collection	Voyage Y6 collection		1 anthology per year of short stories by significant authors differentiated at two levels
		Level 1 16 fiction 4 non-fiction titles RA 6–6.6 **Level 2** 16 fiction 4 non-fiction 2 play titles RA 6.6–7 **Level 3** 16 fiction 4 non-fiction 3 play titles RA 7–7.6 **Level 4** 16 fiction 4 non-fiction 3 play titles RA 7.6–8 **Level 5** 16 fiction 4 non-fiction 3 play titles RA 8–8.6			Revised edition Struggling readers; assessment materials

W

Series Title and Publisher	Features	YR/P1	Y1/P2	Y2/P3
Wellington Square – Think About It Nelson Thornes	T, S, IT Fiction and non-fiction sets			
West African Junior Readers Nelson Thornes	A mixture of fiction and non-fiction in each book			
What's Their Story? OUP see **Oxford Reading Tree Non-fiction**				
White Wolves A&C Black	T, S Fiction			
Wide Range Readers Longman	T A mixture of fiction and non-fiction			

W

Y3/P4	Y4/P5	Y5/P6	Y6/P7	KS3 Older Developing Readers	Comment
		Level 1 2 fiction 2 non-fiction titles RA 6–6.6 **Level 2** 2 fiction 2 non-fiction titles RA 6.6–7 **Level 3** 2 fiction 2 non-fiction titles RA 7–7.6 **Level 4** 2 fiction 2 non-fiction titles RA 7.6–8 **Level 5** 2 fiction 2 non-fiction titles RA 8–8.6			For struggling readers Citizenship themes. Can be used in conjunction with Wellington Square, or stand-alone
Junior Readers 1	Junior Readers 2	Junior Readers 3	Junior Readers 4		Specifically written for children throughout West Africa
3 titles	3 titles	3 titles	3 titles		By significant authors
					Out of print

W

Series Title and Publisher	Features	YR/P1	Y1/P2	Y2/P3
Wildcats Kingscourt/McGraw-Hill	T, S Fiction and non-fiction anthologies			
Wolf Hill OUP	T, S, IT Fiction			
Yellow Bananas Egmont Books see **Bananas**				
Zebras Horwitz Gardner	T, S Non-fiction			Set A 20 titles

Z

Y3/P4	Y4/P5	Y5/P6	Y6/P7	KS3 Older Developing Readers	Comment
		Cougar 12 titles RA 6–7			Anthologies with a wide range of genres
		Lion 12 titles RA 7–8 **Tiger** 12 titles RA 8–9 **Bobcat** 12 titles RA 9–10			
				Leopard 12 titles RA 10–11 **Panther** 12 titles RA 11–12	
		Level 1 12 titles RA 6.6–7 **Level 2** 6 titles RA 7–7.6			For reluctant readers
		Level 3 6 titles RA 7.6–8			
		Level 4 6 titles RA 8–8.6 **Level 5** 6 titles RA 8.6–9			
Set B 20 titles					

Series Title and Publisher	Features	YR/P1	Y1/P2	Y2/P3
Zone 13 Nelson Thornes	Fiction			
Zoom Ginn	T, S Fiction			←

Y3/P4	Y4/P5	Y5/P6	Y6/P7	KS3 Older Developing Readers	Comment
			Level 1 6 titles **Level 2** ← 6 titles → **Level 3** 6 titles RA 8+		For reluctant readers
Sets 1–6 ← 8 titles per set → RA 5–7					For struggling readers **Out of print**

Z

Supplementary List

Series intended for use with reluctant, struggling and older developing readers

Series Title and Publisher	Features	Interest Age 5–7	Interest Age 7–9	Interest Age 9–11	Interest Age 11–14	Comment
4 Aces Football Graphic Novels Ticktock Publishing	IT Fiction			← 4 titles RA8+ →		Boy-friendly For reluctant readers
4U2Read.OK Barrington Stoke	Fiction	← 9 titles (RA below 8) →		← 17 titles (RA below 8) →		Simplified versions of Barrington Stoke novels for reluctant readers by significant authors
Alpha to Omega Heinemann	Highly structured programme from KS2 to adult. Back-up Readers consolidate programme stages. Currently being revised.					
Animals in Danger Ticktock Publishing	Non-fiction		← 4 titles (RA 7+) →			For reluctant readers
Badger Secondary Reading Boxes Badger Publishing	Fiction and non-fiction sets				Breakaway Fiction for Weaker Readers SurefireWinners Novels A Surefire Winners Novels B Fantasy and Sci-fi Group Readers Mysteries Group Readers RA 8–10	For weaker readers Approx. 32 books per set

Series / Publisher	Type	Titles / Reading Age	Notes
Bangers and Mash Longman	T, S Fiction	24 titles 8 Supplementary titles RA 5.6–7.11	Phonic series **Out of print**
Big Machines Franklin Watts	Non-fiction	6 titles RA 6–8	Boy-friendly
Billy Kool Rising Stars		8 titles RA 7–8	Multi-genre books, each containing a non-fiction section
Blitzit Nelson Thornes	T Fiction	**Set A** – 6 titles **Set B** – 6 titles RA 8+	For reluctant readers
Boys Rule! Rising Stars	S Fiction	20 titles RA 7–8	Boy-friendly Short Chapter books with non-fiction section
Brainwaves Badger Publishing		**Set 1 Green** 18 titles **Set 2 Orange** 18 titles **Set 3 Purple** 18 titles **Blue Set** 6 titles RA 6+	High interest, easy-to-read non-fiction
Buzzwords Nelson Thornes	Fiction	**Pack A** – 8 titles **Pack B** – 8 titles **Pack C** – 8 titles RA 8+	For reluctant readers

Series Title and Publisher	Features	Interest Age 5–7	Interest Age 7–9	Interest Age 9–11	Interest Age 11–14	Comment
Chill Outs Horwitz Gardner	Fiction			↕ 15 Titles RA 6.5–8.5		For turned-off readers
Clever Clogs Ticktock Publishing	Non-Fiction			↕ 12 titles RA 8+		For reluctant readers
Colour Crackers Orchard Books	Fiction	↕ 16 titles RA 7				Humorous stories. 16 titles; some tapes available
Colour Jets Collins	Fiction	↕ 15 titles RA 6+				For reluctant readers
Comix A&C Black	S Fiction		20 titles RA 7+			Graphic fiction; boy-friendly
Crunchies Orchard Books	Fiction	↕ **Crazy Camelot** 8 titles **Little Horrors** 8 titles **Raps** 6 titles **Scaredy Cats** 8 titles RA 7+				Suitable for beginner readers and older reluctant readers
Crunchies – Colour Crunchies Orchard Books	Fiction	↕ **Colour Crackers** 16 titles **First Fairy Tales** 8 titles **Scout and Ace** 4 titles **Titchy Witch** 8 titles RA 7+				Suitable for beginner readers and older reluctant readers

Series / Publisher	Genre	Titles / Reading Age	Notes
Crunchies – Super Crunchies Orchard Books	Fiction	Seriously Silly Stories – 12 titles RA 7+	Suitable for beginner readers and older reluctant readers
Danger Zone Franklin Watts	Non-fiction	4 titles RA 5–7	True-life adventure stories
Dark Flight Badger Publishing	T, S Fiction	10 titles RA 6.6–7	Boy-friendly
Dark Man Ransom	T, S, IT Non-fiction	**Set 1** 6 titles **Set 2** 6 titles RA 5–8 approx	Brief stories for teenage reluctant readers
Digitexts Longman	Fiction and non-fiction	4 titles / 4 titles	Interactive CD containing differentiated text with access versions
Download Readers Rising Stars	IT	8 titles RA 6–7 approx	Magazine-style format. Story interspersed with double pages of non-fiction
Extreme Machines Franklin Watts	Non-fiction	4 titles RA 8–10	Magazine-style format
Falconwood Series AMS Educational see Turnaround			

Series Title and Publisher	Features	Interest Age 5–7	Interest Age 7–9	Interest Age 9–11	Interest Age 11–14	Comment
Famous People, Famous Lives Franklin Watts	Biography		←	11 titles RA 6–8		
Five Minute Thrillers Hi-Lo Books LDA	T Fiction				Set 1 – 8 books Set 2 – 8 Books RA 9	Tapes available for many titles
First Flight Badger Publishing	T, S Each set contains fiction, non-fiction, poetry and a playscript		←	Level 1 – 8 titles RA 6 approx Level 2 – 12 titles RA 6.6 approx		Boy-friendly
Freestyle Express Raintree	Non-fiction				**Material Matters** 6 titles **Turbulent Planet** 4 titles **Energy Essentials** 4 titles **Incredible Creatures** 8 titles **Mean Machines** 4 titles **Body Talk** 6 titles **On the Front Line** 6 titles **A Painful History of Medicine** 4 titles	Non-fiction for reluctant readers. Parallel differentiated versions of mainstream Freestyle series

Full Flight Badger Publishing	T, S Varied genres Each set contains 6 fiction titles, 2 non-fiction, 1 poetry and 1 play script		**Full Flight 1 Pack** 10 titles **Full Flight 2 Pack** 10 Titles **Full Flight 3 Pack** 10 Titles RA 7.5–8	**Destination Detectives** 6 titles all sets RA 8	Particularly boy-friendly. Very short books
Fuzzbuzz OUP	T, S, IT Fiction, includes a non-fiction strand at Level 2	**Level 1, 1A, 1B –** 18 titles RA 5–6.6 **Level 2, 2A, 2B –** 18 titles **Level 2 fuzzbuzz facts** 6 titles RA 6–7.11 **Level 3, 3A** RA 8–9.6			A highly structured special needs scheme
Get Real Franklin Watts	Non-fiction		3 titles RA 7–9		True-life adventures
Gigglers Nelson Thornes	T, S, IT Fiction	**Level 1 – 8 titles** **Level 2 – 8 titles** **Level 3 – 8 titles** RA 6–7.6			Humorous fiction for reluctant readers
Girls Rock Rising Stars	S		8 titles RA 7–8		Girl-friendly For reluctant readers Short chapter books with a non-fiction section

Series Title and Publisher	Features	Interest Age 5–7	Interest Age 7–9	Interest Age 9–11	Interest Age 11–14	Comment
gr8reads Barrington Stoke	Fiction				8 titles RA below 8	Tapes also available
Graffix A&C Black	Fiction			28 titles RA 9		Graphic novels for reluctant readers, boy-friendly
High Impact Heinemann	T Fiction, non-fiction and drama sets				**Set A** fiction, non-fiction, plays RA 6–7 **Set B** fiction, non-fiction, plays RA 7–8 **Set C** fiction, non-fiction, plays RA 8–9 **Set D** fiction, non-fiction, plays RA 9–10	**Out of print** Will be discontinued when current stocks are exhausted For reluctant readers, wide range of titles and genres
Highlights Gardner Education	Fiction			**Set 1** 9 titles RA 7–8 **Set 2** 9 titles RA 8–9		

Hi-Lo Books LDA see **Five Minute Thrillers** and **Ten Minute Thrillers**					
Hodder Reading Project Hodder Murray	T, S A mixture of fiction, non-fiction and plays			**Level 2** – 6 titles NC level 2 **Level 3** – 6 titles NC level 3 **Level 4** – 6 titles NC level 4 **Level 5** – 6 titles NC level 5	An intensive catch-up programme
Hotlinks Kingscourt/McGraw-Hill	T, S, IT Anthologies	20 titles RA 5–6.6			Brief anthologies of fiction and non-fiction
I Love Reading Ticktock Publishing	Non-fiction	6 titles NC1–2 6 titles Blue Level NC1			6 titles produced in 3 versions at different levels of text difficulty; also useful for reluctant readers

Series Title and Publisher	Features	Interest Age 5–7	Interest Age 7–9	Interest Age 9–11	Interest Age 11–14	Comment
Impact Heinemann	T Fiction, non-fiction and drama sets				**Set A** fiction, non-fiction, plays RA 6–7 **Set B** fiction, non-fiction, plays RA 7–8 **Set C** fiction, non-fiction, plays RA 8–9 **Set D** fiction, non-fiction, plays RA 9–10	**Out of print** For reluctant readers, wide range of titles and genres
Inclusive Readers David Fulton	T, S, BB Fiction, non-fiction and poetry		Y3 – 3 titles Y4 – 3 titles	Y5 – 3 titles Y6 – 3 titles		Intended for pupils with moderate to severe learning difficulties. 4 levels of photocopiable text, from p scales to NC Level 1, accompany each Big Book. Many aspects of disability represented

Scheme / Publisher	Type	Titles / Levels	Features
Inside Story Ticktock Publishing	Non-fiction	6 titles RA 8–9	Boy-friendly
Infosteps Kingscourt/McGraw-Hill	S, IT Non-fiction	**Set 1** – 20 titles, RA 7–8 **Set 2** – 20 titles, RA 8–9 **Set 3** – 20 titles, RA 9–10 **Set 4** – 20 titles, RA 10–11	Website divided into 4 levels of reading difficulty to match accompanying sets of books
Jets Collins	Fiction	53 titles in print RA 7+	
Jumbo Jets Collins	Fiction	8 titles RA 7+	
Jumpstart Collins	T, S A range of fiction and non-fiction and poetry	**Stage 1 Set A, B, C** – 18 titles RA 5–6 **Stage 2 Set A, B, C** – 18 titles RA 6–7 **Stage 3 Set A, B, C** – 18 titles RA 7–8	Early intervention scheme for less confident readers
Jumpstart Extra Collins	T, S Non-fiction	**Stage 1** – 10 titles RA 5–6 **Stage 2** – 10 titles RA 6–7 **Stage 3** – 10 titles RA 7–8	Vocabulary and themes linked to Jumpstart
Killer Nature Franklin Watts	Non-fiction	6 titles RA 7–9	
Lightning Ginn	T, IT A range of fiction and non-fiction	7 titles per year Text level from NC Working towards level 2 – NC level 5	Differentiated texts, 3 levels in each book

Series Title and Publisher	Features	Interest Age 5–7	Interest Age 7–9	Interest Age 9–11	Interest Age 11–14	Comment
Literacy Land – Genre Range Longman	IT Non-fiction			6 **Access** versions of standard texts per year		Access versions simplified for lower attainers
Literacy Land – Info Trail Longman Non-fiction	IT			6 **Access** versions of standard texts per year		Access versions simplified for lower attainers
Literacy Land – Streetwise Longman	T, IT Fiction			6 **Access** versions of standard texts per year		Access versions simplified for lower attainers
Literacy World Satellites Heinemann	T, S A range of fiction and non-fiction sets		**Stage 1** NC levels 2c–2a **Stage 2** NC level 2a–3c	**Stage 3** NC level 3a–3b **Stage 4** NC level 3a–4c		For weaker readers, part of a differentiated scheme; 9 books per year
Livewire Chillers Hodder Education	Fiction				4 titles – RA 6–7 16 titles – RA 7–8 9 titles – RA 8–9 3 titles – RA 9–10	
Livewire Fiction Hodder Education	Fiction				6 titles – RA 6–7 6 titles – RA 7–8 8 titles – RA 8–9 5 titles – RA 9–10	
Livewire Graphics Hodder Education	T Fiction				8 titles	Highly visual introductions to pre-20th-century literature

Series / Publisher	Genre					Notes
Livewire Non-Fiction Hodder Education	Non-fiction				2 titles – RA 6–7 20 titles – RA 7–8 11 titles – RA 8–9 6 titles – RA 9–10	
Livewire Plays Hodder Education	Plays				4 titles – RA 6–7 11 titles – RA 7–8 2 titles – RA 8–9	
Livewire Real Lives Hodder Education	Biography				3 titles – RA 6–7 18 titles – RA 7–8 42 titles – RA 8–9 6 titles – RA 9–10	
Livewire Shakespeare Graphics Hodder Education	T				8 titles	Accessible graphic Shakespeare to support lower attainers
Longdale Park (Pathways to Literacy) Collins	T Fiction		Y3 – 6 titles Y4 – 6 titles	Y5 – 6 titles Y6 – 6 titles		For less confident readers, part of the Pathways to Literacy series
Mega Machine Drivers Franklin Watts	Non-fiction	6 titles RA 5–7				Boy-friendly
Navigator Max Rigby see Rigby Navigator Max						
New Windmill Heinemann	Fiction				Some Access titles	
No Limits Franklin Watts	Non-fiction			4 titles RA 8–10		Extreme sports

Series Title and Publisher	Features	Interest Age 5–7	Interest Age 7–9	Interest Age 9–11	Interest Age 11–14	Comment
On the Edge Folens	T, S, IT Fiction				**Start-up Level** – 12 titles RA 6–7 **Level A** – 12 titles RA 7–8 **Level B** – 12 titles RA 8–9 **Level C** – 12 titles RA 9–10	Reluctant teenage readers
Oxford Literacy Web Spiders OUP	T A range of fiction and non-fiction in each set		**Y3** – 9 titles RA 6–7 **Y4** – 9 titles RA 7–8	**Y5** – 9 titles RA 8–9 **Y6** – 9 titles RA 9–10		Particularly boy-friendly, many titles could be used at KS3
Pelican Guided Reading and Writing Longman	T A range of fiction and non-fiction titles	4 titles per term, Y1–Y6 — Each book contains 3 texts at different reading levels				Curriculum-linked, differentiated content
Pelican HiLo Readers Longman	T A range of fiction and non-fiction sets	**Early Level** 18 titles RA 6–7		**Level 1** – 18 titles RA 7–8 **Level 2** – 18 titles RA 8–9		For reluctant and struggling readers

Series / Publisher	Type	Levels	Notes
Rainbow Reading Kingscourt/McGraw-Hill	T, S Fiction with tapes	White Series – 20 books and tapes – RA 5–6 Red Series – 20 books and tapes – RA 6–7 Orange Series – 20 books and tapes – RA 7–8 Yellow Series – 20 books and tapes – RA 8–9 Green Series – 20 books and tapes – RA 9–10 Blue Series – 20 books and tapes – RA 10–11 Violet Series – 20 book and tapes – RA 11–12	Audio-assisted learning NB Tapes now replaced by audio CDs
Rapid Heinemann		6 stages NC 1c–3c	A catch-up programme to be published summer 2006
Rex Jones Badger Publishing	T, S Fiction	8 titles RA 6.6–7	Boy-friendly
Rigby Navigator Max Rigby	T, IT Fiction 3 books per year	Brown Band 3 titles – Y3 Grey Band 3 titles – Y4 Blue Band 3 titles – Y5 Red Band 3 titles – Y6	Curriculum-linked catch-up series for lower ability, parallel to Rigby Navigator NC level 2c–4
Sam's Football Stories Brilliant Publications	Fiction	Set 1 – 6 titles RA 6–7 Set 2 – 6 titles RA 7–8	Boy-friendly
Skyways Collins	T, S Fiction	Level 1 – 8 titles – RA 6 approx Level 2 – 8 titles – RA 6.6 Level 3 – 16 titles – RA 7 Level 4 – 16 titles – RA 7.6 Level 5 – 8 titles– RA 8 Level 6 – 8 titles RA 8.6 Level 7 – 8 titles – RA 9	For less able readers, new edition 1998

Series Title and Publisher	Features	Interest Age 5–7	Interest Age 7–9	Interest Age 9–11	Interest Age 11–14	Comment
Shades Evans Publishing	Fiction			← 15 titles →		Short fast-paced novels, for reluctant or disenchanted readers; books have links to websites
Soldiers Life In… Franklin Watts	Non-fiction			← 7 titles RA 7–9 →		Easy reading versions of Armies of the Past series
Sparklers Nelson Thornes	T, S Fiction	Level 1 – 8 titles – RA 6 approx ← Level 2 – 8 titles – RA 6.6 → Level 3 – 8 titles – RA 7 Level 4 – 8 Titles – RA 7.6				For reluctant readers, each level includes 1 assessment book
Sports Zone Nelson Thornes	Fiction			← Level 1 – 6 titles Level 2 – 6 titles Level 3 – 6 titles RA 8+ →		For reluctant readers
Streetwise Longman see Literacy Land						
Tales of Horror Ticktock Publishing	Fiction				6 titles RA 8+	For reluctant readers
Talking About Football Franklin Watts	Non-fiction		← 4 titles RA 6–8 →			Boy-friendly

Series	Type	Titles	Notes
Ten Minute Thrillers LDA	T Fiction	10 titles RA 8	For struggling and reluctant readers. Some tapes also available
Top Cars Franklin Watts		6 titles RA 8–10	Boy-friendly
Trackers OUP	T, S, IT Fiction and non-fiction sets at each level	**Bear Tracks** – 10 titles – RA 5.6 approx **Elephant Tracks** – 10 titles – RA 5.9 **Frog Tracks** – 10 titles – RA 6 **Giraffe Tracks** – 10 titles – RA 6.3 **Parrot Tracks** – 10 titles – RA 6.6 **Tiger Tracks** – 10 titles – RA 6.9 **Zebra Tracks** – 10 titles – RA 7	For struggling readers working within NC level 1–2
Trailblazers Ransom	S, IT	**Set 1** – 3 titles **Set 2** – 3 titles RA 6–7	Approx Each Book has a non-fiction section followed by a story
Turnaround AMS Educational	S Fiction	**Turnaround 1** 12 titles **Turnaround 2** 12 titles **Turnaround Plays Pack 1** 4 titles **Turnaround Plays Pack 2** 4 titles RA 7–9	For reluctant readers, well-known authors

Series Title and Publisher	Features	Interest Age 5–7	Interest Age 7–9	Interest Age 9–11	Interest Age 11–14	Comment
Wellington Square Nelson Thornes	T, S, IT A range of fiction and non-fiction sets at each level		**Level 1** – 16 fiction, 4 non-fiction titles RA 6–6.6 **Level 2** – 16 fiction, 4 non-fiction, 2 play titles RA 6.6–7 **Level 3** – 16 fiction, 4 non-fiction, 3 play titles RA 7–7.6 **Level 4** – 16 fiction, 4 non-fiction, 3 play titles RA 7.6–8 **Level 5** – 16 fiction, 4 non-fiction, 3 play titles RA 8–8.6			Revised edition For struggling readers; assessment materials available
Wellington Square – Think About It Nelson Thornes	T, S, IT Fiction and non-fiction sets		**Level 1** – 2 fiction, 2 non-fiction titles RA 6–6.6 **Level 2** – 2 fiction, 2 non-fiction titles RA 6.6–7 **Level 3** – 2 fiction, 2 non-fiction titles RA 7–7.6 **Level 4** – 2 fiction, 2 non-fiction titles RA 7.6–8 **Level 5** – 2 fiction, 2 non-fiction titles RA 8–8.6			For struggling readers, Citizenship themes. Can be used in conjunction with Wellington Square, or stand-alone
Wildcats Kingscourt/McGraw-Hill	T, S Fiction and non-fiction		**Cougar** 12 titles RA 6–7	**Lion** 12 titles – RA 7–8 **Tiger** 12 titles – RA 8–9 **Bobcat** 12 titles – RA 9–1	**Leopard** 12 titles RA 10–11 **Panther** 12 titles RA 11–12	Anthologies with a wide range of genres

Wolf Hill OUP	T, S, IT Fiction	Level 1 12 titles – RA 6.6–7 Level 2 6 titles – RA 7–7.6 Level 3 6 titles – RA 7.6–8 Level 4 6 titles – RA 8–8.6 Level 5 6 titles – RA 8.6–9	For reluctant readers
World War II Stories Franklin Watts	Non-fiction	4 titles RA 7–9	
Zone 13 Nelson Thornes	Fiction	Level 1 – 6 titles Level 2 – 6 titles Level 3 – 6 titles RA 8+	For reluctant readers
Zoom Ginn	T, S Fiction	6 sets 8 titles per set RA 5–7	**Out of print** For struggling readers

Publishers' Addresses

A&C Black
MDL
Brunel Road
Houndmills
Basingstoke
RG21 6XS
Tel: 01256 302692
www.acblack.com

AMS International
Woodside Trading Estate
Low Lane
Horsforth
Leeds
LS18 5NY
Tel: 0113 258 0309
www.senter.co.uk

Badger Publishing
16 Wedgwood Gate
Pin Green Industrial Estate
Stevenage
Hertfordshire
SG1 4SU
Tel: 01438 356907
www.badger-publishing.co.uk

Barrington Stoke
Sandeman House
Trunk's Close
55 High Street
Edinburgh
EH1 1SR
Tel: 0131 557 2020
www.barringtonstoke.co.uk

Brilliant Publications
BEBC Distribution
Albion Close
Parkstone
Poole
Dorset
BH12 3LL
Tel: 0845 1309200
www.brilliantpublications.co.uk

Cambridge University Press (CUP)
FREEPOST
The Edinburgh Building
Cambridge
CB2 1BR
Tel: 01223 325588
www.cambridge.org/education

Collins Educational
HarperCollins Publishers
FREEPOST GW2446
Glasgow
G64 1BR
Tel: 0870 787 1610 (primary)
     0870 767 1612 (secondary)
www.collinseducation.com

David Fulton Publishers
The Chiswick Centre
414 Chiswick High Road
London
W4 5TF
Tel: 020 8996 3610
www.fultonpublishers.co.uk

Egmont Books
239 Kensington High Street
London
W8 6SA
Tel: 020 7761 3500
www.egmont.co.uk

Evans Publishing
Evans Publishing Group
2A Portman Mansions
Chiltern Street
London
W1U 6NR
Tel: 01264 343072
www.evansbooks.co.uk

Folens
Folens Ltd
Apex Business Centre
Boscombe Road
Dunstable
Bedfordshire
LU5 4RL
Tel: 0870 609 1235
www.folens.com

Franklin Watts
Hachette Childrens Books
338 Euston Road
London
NW1 3BH
Tel: 020 7873 6000
www.franklinwatts.co.uk

Ginn
Customer Services Dept
Ginn and Co
FREEPOST (SCE 6313)
PO Box 970
Oxford
OX2 8BR
Tel: 01865 888000
www.myprimary.co.uk

Handsome Prints
Durrows
Quarry Lane
Kelsall
Cheshire
CW6 0PD
Tel: 01829 751097
Email: KarenTaylor43205@aol.com

HarperCollins Childrens Books
See Collins
www.harpercollinschildrensbooks.co.uk

Heinemann Educational
Customer Services Dept
Heinemann Educational
FREEPOST (SCE 6316)
PO Box 970
Oxford
OX2 8BR
Tel: 01865 888020
www.myprimary.co.uk

Hodder Murray
338 Euston Road
London
NW1 3BH
Tel: 020 7873 6000
www.livewirebooks.co.uk
www.hodder.co.uk

Horwitz Gardner
(renamed **Gardner Education**)
168e High Street
Egham
Surrey
TW20 9HP
Tel: 01784 477470
www.gardner-education.com

Jelly and Bean
15 Mallinson Crescent
Harrogate
North Yorkshire
HG2 9HP
Tel: 01423 879182
www.jellyandbean.co.uk

Jolly Learning Ltd
Tailours House
High Road
Chigwell
Essex
IG7 6DL
Tel: 020 8501 0405
www.jollylearning.co.uk

Kingfisher
Kingfisher Publications plc
New Penderel House
283–288 High Holborn
London
WC1V 7HZ
Tel: 020 7903 9999
www.kingfisherpub.com

Kingscourt/McGraw-Hill
Kingscourt/McGraw-Hill Order Dept
FREEPOST LON16295
Maidenhead
Berkshire
SL6 2BT
Tel: 0800 317 457
www.kingscourt.co.uk

Ladybird
Customer Services
Pearson Customer Operations
Edinburgh Gate
Harlow
Essex
CM20 2JE
Tel: 0870 607 7600
www.ladybird.co.uk

LDA
Duke Street
Wisbech
Cambridgeshire
PE13 2AE
Tel: 01945 463441
www.LDAlearning.com

Letterland International Ltd
Barton
Cambridge
CB3 7AY
Tel: 0870 766 2629
www.letterland.com

Longman
Schools Division
Longman
FREEPOST ANG2041
Harlow
Essex
Tel: 0800 579579
www.longman.co.uk

Neate Publishing
6 Woodgreen Road
Winchester
Hampshire
SO22 6LH
Tel: 01962 620216
www.neatepublishing.co.uk

Nelson Thornes
Customer Services
FREEPOST SWC0507
Cheltenham
Gloucestershire
GL53 7ZZ
Tel: 01242 267280
www.nelsonthornes.com

Orchard Books
Hachette Childrens Books
338 Euston Road
London
NW1 3BH
Tel: 020 7873 6000
www.orchardbooks.co.uk

Oxford University Press (OUP)
Oxford University Press
Educational Supply Section
Saxon Way West
Corby
Northamptonshire
NN18 9ES
Tel: 01536 454519
www.oxfordprimary.com

Puffin (Penguin)
Books on Demand
FREEPOST NATE1108
Harlow
Essex
CM20 2BR
Tel: 0870 6977600
www.puffin.co.uk

Raintree
Raintree Publishers
Halley Court
Jordan Hill
Oxford
OX2 8EJ
Tel: 01865 888112 (primary)
      01865 888113 (secondary)
www.raintreepublishers.co.uk

Ransom
Ransom Publishing Ltd
Rose Cottage
Howe Hill
Watlington
Oxfordshire
OX49 5HB
Tel: 01491 613711
www.ransom.co.uk

Read Write Inc
See OUP
www.ruthmiskin.literacy.com

Rigby
Customer Services Dept
Rigby Educational Publishers
FREEPOST (SCE 6316)
PO Box 970
Oxford
OX2 8BR
Tel: 01865 888044
www.myprimary.co.uk

Rising Stars
PO Box 5948
Wellingborough
Northamptonshire
NN8 2FD
Tel: 01933 443862
www.risingstars-uk.com

Ticktock Publishing
Ticktock Direct Ltd
FREEPOST Unit 2
Orchard Business Centre
North Farm Road
Tunbridge Wells
Kent
TN2 3XF
Tel: 0870 381 2223
www.ticktock.co.uk

CD inside
CD inside
CD inside
CD inside
CD inside

Every Child
Matters:
A New Role
for SENCOs

Every Child Matters
A New Role for SENCOs

A practical guide

What will the
SENCO role be in
schools of the
future?

Practical strategies
for effecting
change

Preparing for
OFSTED

RITA CHEMINAIS

David Fulton Publishers

Available Now!

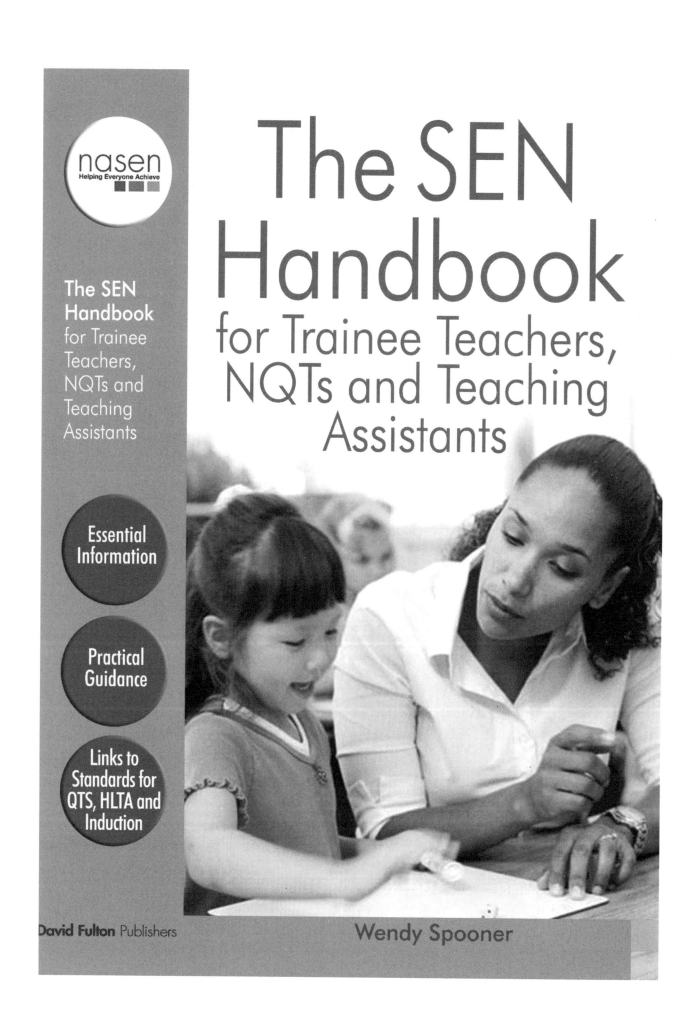

The SEN Handbook for Trainee Teachers, NQTs and Teaching Assistants

Essential Information

Practical Guidance

Links to Standards for QTS, HLTA and Induction

The SEN Handbook for Trainee Teachers, NQTs and Teaching Assistants

David Fulton Publishers

Wendy Spooner

Available Now!